DRUG ADDICTION AND RECOVERY

Marijuana and Synthetics

DRUG ADDICTION AND RECOVERY

Marijuana and Synthetics

John Perritano

SERIES CONSULTANT
SARA BECKER, Ph.D.
Brown University School of Public Health
Warren Alpert Medical School

MASON CREST

Mason Crest
450 Parkway Drive, Suite D
Broomall, PA 19008
www.masoncrest.com

MTM Publishing, Inc.
www.mtmpublishing.com

President: Valerie Tomaselli
Vice President, Book Development: Hilary Poole
Designer: Annemarie Redmond
Copyeditor: Peter Jaskowiak
Editorial Assistant: Andrea St. Aubin

Series ISBN: 978-1-4222-3598-0
Hardback ISBN: 978-1-4222-3606-2
E-Book ISBN: 978-1-4222-8250-2

Cataloging-in-Publication Data on file with the Library of Congress

Printed and bound in the United States of America.

First printing
9 8 7 6 5 4 3 2 1

TABLE OF CONTENTS

Key Icons to Look for:

Words to Understand: These words with their easy-to-understand definitions will increase the reader's understanding of the text, while building vocabulary skills.

Sidebars: This boxed material within the main text allows readers to build knowledge, gain insights, explore possibilities, and broaden their perspectives by weaving together additional information to provide realistic and holistic perspectives.

Research Projects: Readers are pointed toward areas of further inquiry connected to each chapter. Suggestions are provided for projects that encourage deeper research and analysis.

Text-Dependent Questions: These questions send the reader back to the text for more careful attention to the evidence presented there.

Educational Videos: Readers can view videos by scanning our QR codes, providing them with additional educational content to supplement the text. Examples include news coverage, moments in history, speeches, iconic sports moments and much more!

Series Glossary of Key Terms: This back-of-the-book glossary contains terminology used throughout the series. Words found here increase the reader's ability to read and comprehend higher-level books and articles in this field.

SERIES INTRODUCTION

Many adolescents in the United States will experiment with alcohol or other drugs by time they finish high school. According to a 2014 study funded by the National Institute on Drug Abuse, about 27 percent of 8th graders have tried alcohol, 20 percent have tried drugs, and 13 percent have tried cigarettes. By 12th grade, these rates more than double: 66 percent of 12th graders have tried alcohol, 50 percent have tried drugs, and 35 percent have tried cigarettes.

Adolescents who use substances experience an increased risk of a wide range of negative consequences, including physical injury, family conflict, school truancy, legal problems, and sexually transmitted diseases. Higher rates of substance use are also associated with the leading causes of death in this age group: accidents, suicide, and violent crime. Relative to adults, adolescents who experiment with alcohol or other drugs progress more quickly to a full-blown substance use disorder and have more co-occurring mental health problems.

The National Survey on Drug Use and Health (NSDUH) estimated that in 2015 about 1.3 million adolescents between the ages of 12 and 17 (5 percent of adolescents in the United States) met the medical criteria for a substance use disorder. Unfortunately, the vast majority of these

IF YOU NEED HELP NOW . . .

SAMHSA's National Helpline provides referrals for mental-health or substance-use counseling.
1-800-662-HELP (4357) or https://findtreatment.samhsa.gov

SAMHSA's National Suicide Prevention Lifeline provides crisis counseling by phone or online, 24-hours-a-day and 7 days a week.
1-800-273-TALK (8255) or http://www.suicidepreventionlifeline.org

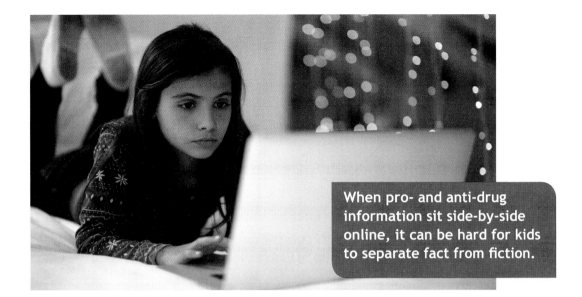

When pro- and anti-drug information sit side-by-side online, it can be hard for kids to separate fact from fiction.

adolescents did not receive treatment. Less than 10 percent of those with a diagnosis received specialty care, leaving 1.2 million adolescents with an unmet need for treatment.

The NSDUH asked the 1.2 million adolescents with untreated substance use disorders why they didn't receive specialty care. Over 95 percent said that they didn't think they needed it. The other 5 percent reported challenges finding quality treatment that was covered by their insurance. Very few treatment providers and agencies offer substance use treatment designed to meet the specific needs of adolescents. Meanwhile, numerous insurance plans have "opted out" of providing coverage for addiction treatment, while others have placed restrictions on what is covered.

Stigma about substance use is another serious problem. We don't call a person with an eating disorder a "food abuser," but we use terms like "drug abuser" to describe individuals with substance use disorders. Even treatment providers often unintentionally use judgmental words, such as describing urine screen results as either "clean" or "dirty." Underlying this language is the idea that a substance use disorder is some kind of moral failing or character flaw, and that people with these disorders deserve blame or punishment for their struggles.

And punish we do. A 2010 report by CASA Columbia found that in the United States, 65 percent of the 2.3 million people in prisons and jails met medical criteria for a substance use disorder, while another 20 percent had histories of substance use disorders, committed their crimes while under the influence of alcohol or drugs, or committed a substance-related crime. Many of these inmates spend decades in prison, but only 11 percent of them receive any treatment during their incarceration. Our society invests significantly more money in punishing individuals with substance use disorders than we do in treating them.

At a basic level, the ways our society approaches drugs and alcohol—declaring a "war on drugs," for example, or telling kids to "Just Say No!"—reflect a misunderstanding about the nature of addiction. The reality is that addiction is a disease that affects all types of people—parents and children, rich and poor, young and old. Substance use disorders stem from a complex interplay of genes, biology, and the environment, much like most physical and mental illnesses.

The way we talk about recovery, using phrases like "kick the habit" or "breaking free," also misses the mark. Substance use disorders are chronic, insidious, and debilitating illnesses. Fortunately, there are a number of effective treatments for substance use disorders. For many patients, however, the road is long and hard. Individuals recovering from substance use disorders can experience horrible withdrawal symptoms, and many will continue to struggle with cravings for alcohol or drugs. It can be a daily struggle to cope with these cravings and stay abstinent. A popular saying at Alcoholics Anonymous (AA) meetings is "one day at a time," because every day of recovery should be respected and celebrated.

There are a lot of incorrect stereotypes about individuals with substance use disorders, and there is a lot of false information about the substances, too. If you do an Internet search on the term "marijuana," for instance, two top hits are a web page by the National Institute on Drug Abuse and a page operated by Weedmaps, a medical and recreational marijuana dispensary. One of these pages publishes scientific information and one publishes pro-marijuana articles. Both pages have a high-quality, professional appearance. If you had never heard of either organization, it would be hard to know which to trust. It can be really difficult for the average person, much less the average teenager, to navigate these waters.

The topics covered in this series were specifically selected to be relevant to teenagers. About half of the volumes cover the types of drugs that they are most likely to hear about or to come in contact with. The other half cover important issues related to alcohol and other drug use (which we refer to as "drug use" in the titles for simplicity). These books cover topics such as the causes of drug use, the influence of drug use on the family, drug use and the legal system, drug use and mental health, and treatment options. Many teens will either have personal experience with these issues or will know someone who does.

This series was written to help young people get the facts about common drugs, substance use disorders, substance-related problems, and recovery. Accurate information can help adolescents to make better decisions. Students who are educated can help each other to better understand the risks and consequences of drug use. Facts also go a long way to reducing the stigma associated with substance use. We tend to fear or avoid things that we don't understand. Knowing the facts can make it easier to support each other. For students who know someone struggling with a substance use disorder, these books can also help them know what to expect. If they are worried about someone, or even about themselves, these books can help to provide some answers and a place to start.

—Sara J. Becker, Ph.D., Assistant Professor (Research), Center for Alcohol and Addictions Studies, Brown University School of Public Health, Assistant Professor (Research), Department of Psychiatry and Human Behavior, Brown University Medical School

WORDS TO UNDERSTAND

cannabinoids: organic chemicals that are the active substances in cannabis plants.

euphoric: a feeling of great happiness.

hallucinating: seeing things that aren't there.

psychedelic: relating to the effects caused by hallucinogenic drugs.

psychoactive: substances that have an effect on mood or behavior.

synthetic: made by humans, rather than occurring in nature.

CHAPTER ONE

WHAT IS MARIJUANA?

Marijuana is one of the most widely consumed drugs in the world. Only alcohol and tobacco are more popular. Although many countries and a few U.S. states have made it legal to sell and smoke marijuana, there is still a lot of disagreement about the drug's effects. Some say it should be legal everywhere, while others say it is too addictive. Some argue it is not harmful, while some insist it is.

Regardless of these disagreements, the plant has a long and storied history as one of the earliest cultivated crops in human history. Marijuana comes from the flowering tops and leaves of two species of plants called *Cannabis sativa* and *Cannabis indica*. Both species produce hemp, the fiber used in rope and other products.

Most experts say the cannabis plant first evolved some 12,000 years ago in Central Asia in what is now Mongolia and southern Siberia. It was the Chinese, however, who first cultivated the crop around 5,000 years ago. They used cannabis as a treatment for rheumatism, gout, and malaria,

11

Foliage of the cannabis plant.

among other maladies. They also used the plant as an anesthetic during surgery. The Chinese brought cannabis to Korea around 2000 BCE, and the plant later spread across South Asia.

As the plant spread, so did its popularity. Many found the leaves had **euphoric** qualities. In India, for example, the plant was used solely for its intoxicating effects. Elsewhere, some followers of Islam smoked the plant instead of drinking alcohol. They learned how to collect the resin drops that coat its leaves and flowers and turned it into hashish, a more powerful form of cannabis.

No one knows exactly when hashish was first discovered, but some stories say it was around 1115 CE. According to legend, an Islamic monk in Persia (modern-day Iran) named Hayder was depressed. He took a walk out into the field and sampled the leaves of the cannabis plant. When he returned to the monastery, Hayder was amazed at how happy he was. His followers asked him why he was so giddy. He told them about the leaves he ate and made them promise they would not reveal the secret. Eventually, of course, the secret got out, and over time people pressed the resin into blocks of hashish. It eventually spread throughout Persia and North Africa.

Marijuana eventually made its way into Europe. Germanic tribes cultivated the plant and took it with them to Britain and other areas. The Vikings in Scandinavia used cannabis as a pain reliever during childbirth and as a remedy for toothaches. The plant then gradually made its way to South America and into North America.

Today, cannabis is grown in almost all types of climates. It flourishes in areas that have abundant sunshine and plenty of water. When dried, marijuana is usually green or brown. It often resembles the popular kitchen spice oregano. Pot, as marijuana is often called, can have a strong smell, or it can have none at all. However, when set ablaze, pot usually has a very specific smell, a bit like burning incense. The primary **psychoactive** ingredient in natural pot is tetrahydrocannabinol (THC).

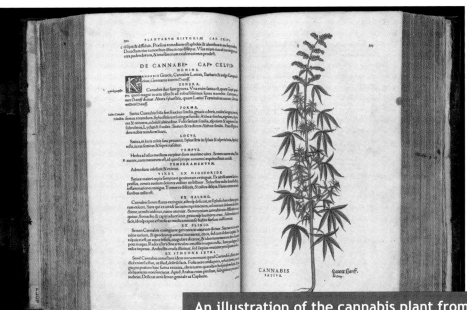

An illustration of the cannabis plant from *Historia Stirpium* (1542) by Leonhart Fuchs, who is considered one of the fathers of botany.

THE WORLD'S LARGEST CANNABIS PRODUCER

Afghanistan is the world's largest producer of cannabis, according to the United Nations Office on Drugs and Crime (UNODC). The nation, which borders Pakistan and Iran, produces between 24,710 and 59,305 acres of cannabis a year. Although several other countries have more land under cultivation, no one tops Afghanistan's estimated annual yield of 1,500 to 3,500 tons of cannabis.

HOORAY FOR HEMP

In addition to its intoxicating effects, cannabis plants have played an important role in the development of civilization. Our early ancestors found out that when woven and twisted together as a rope, cannabis fibers—called hemp—were unbelievably strong and malleable. The rope was so strong that it could be used to pull, drag, and fasten all sorts of things. People could tie it into knots, which they then used to shape nets, snares, and traps for capturing fish and other food.

Hemp was especially important in colonial America. The British first brought cannabis seeds to the New World and ordered colonial farmers to grow the plants. By the 1600s, hemp had become an important crop in New England, Maryland, and Virginia. The colonies grew the plant to make rope, canvas sacks, and paper. Most of the finished products were then sent to Britain to be sold.

When America won its independence from England in 1776, the new U.S. government compelled farmers to grow hemp to bolster the fledgling economy. Some Americans even used hemp to pay their taxes. Rope made from homegrown hemp was vital to the shipping industry as rigging for tall ships. George Washington grew hemp and encouraged others to follow his example.

Today, hemp is still an important commodity, and it is often used in a broad range of products, including home insulation, milk, seeds, lotions, and oils, although its cultivation in the United States is illegal. Most hemp products come from overseas and Canada. Industrial hemp has a lower THC level than the cannabis people smoke.

From Germany, a bag of hemp straw for rodent pets.

THC AND CANNABIS

Scientists believe that **cannabinoids**, which give cannabis its effect, are important tools that help the plants survive. Scientists once thought cannabinoid compounds were produced by the plants as waste products. They now believe the compounds are defense mechanisms, since the taste and fragrance of the cannabinoids discourage insects and other plant-eating animals from destroying the plant before it produces seeds. Moreover, the plant releases cannabinoids into the soil, which discourages other plants from germinating too close and competing for valuable space, water, and nutrients.

MARIJUANA AND CULTURE

Marijuana has also had an enormous impact on popular culture. It has been the focus of hundreds of movies, songs, and TV shows in the United States and other countries. One of the first movies about marijuana was released in 1936. Now a cult classic, the film *Reefer Madness* wildly exaggerated the dangers of marijuana. The goal of the movie was to warn parents, as the movie poster suggested, about "the daily scourge that drags our children into the quagmires of degradation."

In 1969 marijuana was front and center at one of the most famous music events in history—Woodstock. More than 500,000 people gathered at Max Yasgur's farm in Bethel, New York, to take part in the rock concert, billed as "three days of peace, love and music." At the time, reporters indicated that 90 percent of the people at the concert were smoking pot. That same year, the actors Peter Fonda and Dennis Hopper starred in *Easy Rider*, a movie about two motorcyclists taking a cross-country trip filled with marijuana and LSD, a **psychedelic** drug. In an interview 30 years later, Fonda admitted the actors used real marijuana during the filming of at least one scene.

A scene from the 1936 film *Reefer Madness*.

In the 1970s, the sophomoric comedy *Up in Smoke* catapulted pot once again to the center of popular culture. More recent works, such as *Pineapple Express* (2008) and Showtime's hit TV series *Weeds* (2005–2012), about a dope-dealing mother of two, have also drawn huge audiences.

Pot is also a popular topic for artists, writers, and musicians. In 2005, researchers studied 279 popular songs and found that 33.3 percent referenced substance use, mostly alcohol, tobacco, or marijuana. Of that number, 13.6 percent of the songs specifically depicted marijuana use, and 68 percent of the songs portrayed drug use in a positive light.

These days, pot has become more accepted in mainstream culture, and many states have legalized the drug. *Cannabis Planet TV* is a good example of how attitudes regarding marijuana have changed since the *Reefer Madness* days. The 30-minute TV show offers all kinds of information about cannabis, including its history, recipes, music, medicine, and culture. Some people have grown increasingly critical of pot's representation in mainstream culture. Pop culture tends to portray marijuana as a totally harmless drug, ignoring its potential for harm.

SYNTHETIC MARIJUANA

"Weed," another of the nicknames of marijuana, conjures images of a natural product that is harmless. Yet teens and others have discovered a marijuana-like product that it is neither natural nor harmless.

Samuel Alvarado Jr. was 26 years old when his parents rushed him to Denver Health Medical Center in 2013. At the time, the Colorado Department of Public Health and Environment was investigating an outbreak of illnesses related to **synthetic** marijuana, nicknamed "spice." Officials said that three people had died and 75 others were sickened after ingesting a highly potent version of the designer drug.

After buying the drug at a small grocery store, Alvarado began **hallucinating**. He first thought he was walking a dog. He then started arguing with people that weren't there. "I really thought he was going to die," his father told the *Denver Post*. "He was just crazy."

Alvarado recovered, but health-related incidents involving synthetic marijuana, which is made of dried herbs sprayed with chemicals, have continued. In 2015, seven people in Hampton, Virginia, overdosed on synthetic marijuana. One person, a female, died. Officials in Mississippi and Alabama reported that more than 300 people had to be rushed to the emergency room after overdosing on the drug in April 2015. The same thing happened the following November to 13 people in San Diego, California.

From one end of the country to the other, the use of synthetic marijuana has grown tremendously since it first came on the scene. It is a very popular

Spice is sold as an "herbal" substitute for pot, but there is nothing "all natural" about it.

drug among American teenagers. Most people try synthetic marijuana because they think it is just like the real marijuana. Eleven percent of high school seniors admitted to using the drug in 2012 as a "safe" or "natural" alternative to pot. But this is a misunderstanding of what spice actually is.

Sold in slick packaging, "fake marijuana," as it is sometimes called, contains chemicals called cannabinoids, just like natural marijuana does. However, in synthetic marijuana, the cannabinoids are 100 times stronger than THC.

Meanwhile, there are additional chemicals in synthetic marijuana. What these chemicals are can vary from product to product, which means users likely have no idea what they're smoking. But we do know that some of the chemicals in synthetic marijuana are so potent that a person who uses them can become violent, delusional, or anxious. In the United States, the five most commonly used chemicals in synthetic marijuana are illegal because of their psychological effects.

TEXT-DEPENDENT QUESTIONS

1. What is THC?
2. Which society first cultivated marijuana?
3. What are some of the uses for hemp?

RESEARCH PROJECT

Research the top 10 states where marijuana use is the highest. Data can be found on the website of the Substance Abuse and Mental Health Services Administration (http://archive.samhsa.gov/data/NSDUH/2k12State/ NSDUHsae2012/Index.aspx). Next, research the top states where pot is grown. Create a chart and compare the two. What can you conclude?

WORDS TO UNDERSTAND

carcinogens: substances that cause cancer.

extract: to obtain one substance from another.

hippocampus: part of the brain associated with memory and emotions.

severity: level of intensity or seriousness.

CHAPTER TWO

THE SCIENCE OF MARIJUANA

They were young. They were athletic. And they were high. On an early Wednesday morning in November 2015, two policemen at the University of Georgia were patrolling a parking lot when they spotted a vehicle with its lights on. As they approached, they noticed a plume of smoke inside the vehicle.

After asking the two occupants to step out of the car, officers noticed what looked like a "pile of loose tobacco" sitting on the ground near the passenger-side door. "When the door opened, the cloud of smoke came out along with the strong odor of burnt marijuana," one of the officers wrote. Police also found a jar with what they suspected to be a "bud" of green marijuana.

Police arrested the car's two occupants, both freshmen football players. The players were automatically suspended from the next game. While pot smoking in college seldom makes headlines (unless students are arrested, of course), researchers from the Monitoring the Future (MTF) study, run by the

A young man at Hempfest in Seattle, 2012.

National Institute on Drug Abuse (NIDA), say that nearly 6 percent of college students that they surveyed in 2014 admitted to smoking marijuana at least 20 times in the previous month. This was the highest rates of marijuana smoking since 1980.

"It's clear that for the past seven or eight years there has been an increase in marijuana use among the nation's college students," the study's lead researcher said. "This largely parallels an increase we have been seeing among high school seniors." Yet while more college students are using marijuana, overall marijuana usage either has held steady or · decreased over the past several years, especially among teenagers. The MTF study annually surveys about 40,000 students in the 8th, 10th, and 12th grades. In 2015 the MTF reported that lifetime marijuana use was down slightly over the previous year for all grade levels. In 2015, 15.50

percent of 8th graders reported that they had used marijuana during the previous year, down from 15.60 percent in 2014. The percentages also dropped for 10th graders (31.10 from 33.70). Among 12th graders, however, there was a slight uptick in use (44.70 from 44.40).

Meanwhile, from 2014 to 2015, the past monthly use of marijuana among 8th, 10th, and 12th graders held steady, with 8th graders at 6.5 percent, 10th graders at 16.6 percent, and 12th graders at 21.2 percent. According to the MTF survey, most teens don't seem too concerned about any harmful consequences associated with marijuana use. In 2014, 31.9 percent of seniors believed regular marijuana use was harmful, down from 36.1 percent the previous year. Moreover, 81 percent of high school seniors say it is not hard to obtain marijuana.

In addition, there is an increasing trend in the percentage of teenagers consuming marijuana in edible forms, such as in cookies, brownies, and other products. The increase in these so-called edibles is especially high in states that have legalized marijuana (40 percent) compared to other states

According to the Monitoring the Future survey, roughly 1 in 5 high school seniors use marijuana.

(26 percent). Interestingly, there was only a small increase in 2014 in the rates of marijuana use by seniors in states where pot has been legalized (34.5 percent) compared with states where it hasn't been (30.1 percent). Researchers point to early prevention efforts as the reason marijuana use has declined over the past few years.

HOW PEOPLE USE MARIJUANA

A person can ingest marijuana in a variety of ways. Most people smoke marijuana by either rolling it in cigarette paper or using a pipe or a bong (water pipe). Some people also smoke "blunts," which are made by emptying a cigar of its tobacco and refilling it partially with marijuana. Smoking marijuana is the most common method of using the drug, although there are concerns that marijuana smoke can hurt the lungs.

Some people use vaporizers, which **extract** the active ingredients from the leaves and collect them in a vapor storage unit. A person then inhales the vapor, not the smoke. Some people even mix marijuana with certain foods, including brownies and cookies (known as "edibles"). Others brew it as a tea. A new method of use is smoking or eating different forms of TCH-rich resins,

ATHLETIC PERFORMANCE

Evidence suggests that using marijuana can have a negative impact on athletic performance. Pot impacts a person's coordination, reaction time, and concentration—all tools that athletes need to compete. It can also make an athlete, or anyone else for that matter, more tired. Because marijuana is stored in body fat, its effects can be long-lasting. Some studies have found that impairment can last as long as 24 hours after marijuana usage.

Cannabis can be put into edible products like candy and cookies.

a practice called "dabbing." This method allows a person to intake large amounts of THC. But preparing the extracts can be dangerous. A person has to use a butane lighter, which can cause a fire and serious burn injuries.

THE CHEMISTRY OF MARIJUANA

Marijuana contains more than 60 cannabinoids, the most powerful of which is THC. All of us have natural cannabinoids in our bodies that affect the central nervous system. These chemicals fine-tune how our neurons, or brain cells, communicate with one another. When a person smokes marijuana, the THC quickly makes its way from the lungs to the blood stream. The blood then carries the chemical to the brain and other organs. The amount of THC in pot determines how "high" a person gets. Dried marijuana contains between 2 and 20 percent THC.

Although marijuana has been around for centuries, it wasn't until the 1990s that scientists began to understand how marijuana affected the human body. One of the most important discoveries was the existence of a special communication network called the endocannabinoid (EC) system.

Inside the EC system are special receptor cells that uptake cannabinoids and change the body's chemistry. In the brain's **hippocampus**, for example, millions of cannabinoid receptors bind with THC, influencing how the cells send, receive, and process messages.

It is in the hippocampus that scientists believe marijuana produces its high. The hippocampus is responsible for driving our emotions and our short- and long-term memory. When THC overwhelms the receptor cells, it interferes with the ability of the natural cannabinoids to do their jobs.

EFFECTS ON THE BODY

The effects of THC can literally be mind-numbing. The users' reaction times slow down, and users may have trouble remembering things that just happened. Their coordination is thrown off, as is their attention span. THC also makes a person feel good—the "high" associated with marijuana.

Each person reacts differently to THC. The cannabinoid can sometimes make people laugh uncontrollably. It can make them talkative, or silent. Those high on TCH might experience dry mouth and eyes. They might get hungry. A few hours after smoking, they might become sleepy. And while pot makes some users feel good, others become anxious or panicky. There are also a number of physical effects. Marijuana smoke can irritate the lining of the lungs, causing breathing problems. Marijuana also raises a person's heart rate by 20 to 50 percent within minutes.

Marijuana smoking poses some risk for people who might have heart problems. A 2015 study by the Harvard Medical School and Boston's Beth Israel Deaconess Medical Center concluded that pot smokers are five times more likely to suffer a heart attack than nonsmokers. The researchers believe the drug puts an added strain on the heart, although they are not sure whether THC is the main culprit. It was the first study to link marijuana with heart attacks.

POT AND PREGNANCY

Although THC and other cannabinoids are not toxic, they do have the potential to harm unborn children if women smoke while they are pregnant. We say "potential," because there is considerable disagreement among doctors and scientists as to the extent and severity of the problem. There is little evidence to suggest that marijuana use by pregnant mothers results in low birth weight or birth defects. It is known that THC can be passed from mothers to their children while in the womb or while breast-feeding, but scientists do not fully understand the consequences of THC exposure during pregnancy.

Among other things, researchers found there was "mixed" evidence to support a link between marijuana use and birth defects. They also said there was "insufficient" evidence that offspring of mothers who were using pot while pregnant are more likely to use pot themselves as they get older. However, the American Academy of Pediatrics reported in 2013 that maternal marijuana use could result in behavior and attention problems when a child gets older.

Scientists are not sure of the effects of cannabis on unborn babies.

Previous research has shown that marijuana causes an increase in heart rate along with fluctuations in blood pressure. It also decreases the blood's ability to carry oxygen, forcing the heart to work harder, which increases the risk of heart attack.

POT ON THE BRAIN

For teens, pot can create long-term problems. It interferes with a student's normal brain function, decreasing their motivation, memory, and ability to pay attention. During the teenage years, a person's brain is still forming, as its various parts try to connect with one another. Smoking pot can derail that process.

In the 1980s, scientists linked cannabis use to cognitive defects in rats. Rats that were given cannabis in adolescence showed signs of learning and memory impairment as adults. A 2012 study in found that habitual pot use at a young age corresponded to lower intelligence in adulthood.

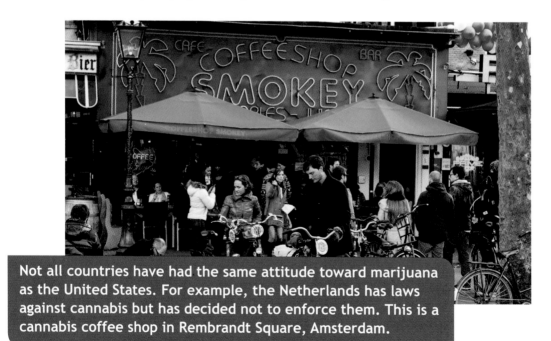

Not all countries have had the same attitude toward marijuana as the United States. For example, the Netherlands has laws against cannabis but has decided not to enforce them. This is a cannabis coffee shop in Rembrandt Square, Amsterdam.

Researchers from Duke University found that those who smoked pot frequently in their early teens had a six-point drop in their IQ by the time they reached 38. Individuals who started using pot heavily as adults did not show the same results. Moreover, the brain function of those who smoked pot consistently in their teens did not improve if they quit.

Critics of the research argue that these results might not have anything to do with pot smoking. They point out that the studies did not "control" for a number of other variables, like economic status, parental level of education, and other risky behaviors such as heavy drinking. The argument is that people who are more likely to smoke as teenagers might also be more likely to live in poor communities, come from less educated families, and engage in other risky behaviors. These variables, rather than marijuana smoking, might be responsible for the drop in IQ. A 2014 study at University College London (UCL) appeared to provide some support for this argument. This study followed 2,612 children born in the United Kingdom and found that early marijuana smoking did not have any effect on IQ when variables like maternal education, cigarette use, and alcohol use were controlled for in the analysis.

A 2014 report in the *Journal of Neuroscience* compared brain scans of 18- to 25-year-olds who smoked marijuana at least once a week with those who did not. Researchers found that the brains of pot smokers were significantly altered. Using magnetic resonance imaging, researchers found that the part of the brain involved with processing rewards was much larger in pot smokers compared with nonsmokers. The more a person smoked, the greater the abnormalities.

A review of the negative health effects of pot smoking in 2014 by the *New England Journal of Medicine* concluded that smoking pot regularly from an early age results in a lower IQ. In the journal, Dr. Nora Volkow, the director of NIDA, and some of her colleagues stated that "the evidence suggests that such use [heavy marijuana use as a teenager] results in measurable and long-lasting cognitive impairments."

THE EFFECTS OF "SPICE"

While pot can relax a person, synthetic marijuana can have the opposite effect. Like marijuana, people intake "spice" by smoking or consuming the drug. Sometimes they mix spice with natural marijuana, and sometimes they brew it as a tea. Others inhale vaporized synthetic cannabinoid liquids in e-cigarettes.

MYTHS AND FACTS ABOUT POT AND HEALTH

Myth: Pot use causes cancer.

Facts: This is murky. A 2006 study by researchers at the University of California, Los Angeles (UCLA) concluded that while marijuana smoke does contain several **carcinogens**, it does not lead to cancer. The study looked at 1,209 patients with lung, oral, and respiratory-tract cancers. Researchers found no correlation between marijuana and these diseases. While there is no direct evidence linking pot smoking to cancer, there's also no hard evidence to suggest it doesn't.

Myth: Pot kills off brain cells.

Facts: Although pot can change the brain's structure and limit its function, it does not kill brain cells. Heavy pot users often find their short-term memory has been impaired. They also are less motivated and have less energy.

Myth: No one has died from using marijuana.

Facts: Daily pot smokers are 30 percent more likely to have an accident than nonsmokers. In Baltimore, a study found that out of 1,023 emergency room patients, 34.7 percent were under the influence of marijuana. Because marijuana impacts motor control, short-term memory, concentration, and judgment, pot can theoretically kill under the right circumstances, such as driving a car while under the influence.

Since spice is a relatively new drug, researchers are only beginning to understand how it affects the brain. What they do know is that the chemicals found in the drug affect the same parts of the brain as THC. However, the chemicals are much more efficient at binding to receptors in the brain than THC is. In addition, the chemicals are much more potent. This combination of being more efficient *and* more potent can create extremely strong and life-threatening side effects. Some people might become relaxed after smoking synthetic marijuana, but they might hallucinate instead. They might also become agitated, delusional, have seizures, or start vomiting uncontrollably.

TEXT-DEPENDENT QUESTIONS

1. What are three main ways that people can ingest marijuana?
2. What is the endocannabinoid (EC) system, and how does it work?
3. What are the facts about pot and cancer?

RESEARCH PROJECT

Create a computer slide show with pictures and text that highlights the various physical and mental effects of marijuana use.

WORDS TO UNDERSTAND

coalesce: to gather around or unite.

decriminalized: something that is not technically legal but is no longer subject to prosecution.

disparities: significant differences, often resulting in a lack of equality.

recreational: something done for enjoyment only; here, "recreational" drug use is contrasted with drug use for medical purposes.

CHAPTER THREE

THE DEBATE OVER LEGALIZATION

Attitudes regarding marijuana have changed drastically over the past several years. As a country, our days of *Reefer Madness* seem to have passed. Today, 37 states plus the District of Columbia have liberalized their marijuana laws. Some states have **decriminalized** pot. This means that while pot is still illegal in the state, the courts will not prosecute a person for possessing small amounts of it. A person won't go to jail and won't receive a criminal record. Nineteen states have decriminalized marijuana laws.

Other states have legalized marijuana for **recreational** and medical use. In other words, it is legal to buy marijuana in those states under strict guidelines. In Oregon, Washington, the District of Columbia, Colorado, and Alaska, marijuana is a legal recreational and medicinal drug. (Experts say it is likely that number will increase after the 2016 elections.) In other states, such as New York, Connecticut, and Illinois, only medical marijuana is legal.

CRIMINALIZING MARIJUANA

The current movement to legalize marijuana is in stark contrast to the effort to criminalize it in 1970. That year, when law and order were on the minds of most Americans, President Richard Nixon implored Congress to crack down on drug use by passing the Controlled Substances Act of 1970. The law imposed stiff penalties for the use and sale of illegal drugs. At the time, many lawmakers believed that marijuana made people do things they normally wouldn't do. It was *Reefer Madness* all over again.

During the debate, Senator Thomas Dodd of Connecticut, the chief sponsor of the bill, held up a package that he said contained $3,000 worth of marijuana. He then went on to tell his colleagues that marijuana had caused a U.S. Army sergeant fighting during the Vietnam War to suffer such "dreadful hallucinations" that he called down a mortar strike on his own troops.

The measure passed handily, although some senators tried to derail the proposal because the penalties were so stiff. "We should not subject our

Narcotics agents pose with over 400 pounds of marijuana after a major drug bust in 1963.

Two New York City college students hide their faces from the media after being arrested for pot possession in 1968.

citizens, particularly our young people, to the penalties in this bill," argued Senator Harold E. Hughes of Iowa, "in part because of the conditions of our jails and prisons," which he added were more dangerous than the drug.

The law immediately listed marijuana as a Schedule I drug, alongside more dangerous and potent substances such as LSD and heroin. That law is still in effect today. Penalties for possessing and selling Schedule I drugs are severe. A first-time offender found with 1 to 49 marijuana plants could expect jail time of not more than 5 years and a fine not exceeding more than $250,000. If convicted a second time, a person could be sentenced to at least 10 years in prison and fined $500,000. A person possessing 50 kilograms or less of marijuana or less than 10 kilograms of hashish can expect to spend not more than 5 years in prison on the first offense and 10 years for a second offense.

Under public pressure, states have begun to rethink their marijuana laws in recent years. New York once had the toughest drug laws of any state. Known as the Rockefeller Drug Laws, a person possessing at least 4

RACE, ETHNICITY, AND MARIJUANA LAWS

In the opinion of many historians, the move in the United States to criminalize marijuana in the early 20th century was prompted by efforts to curb Mexican immigration into the United States. At the time, police officers in the Southwest claimed that Mexican immigrants were selling the "killer weed" to American school children. Police even said pot was responsible for an upsurge in violent crimes.

In New Orleans, the public joined in the paranoia. Newspapers decried marijuana, too, declaring it was used by African Americans, musicians, prostitutes, and other nefarious criminals. Those who campaigned against the drug called it a menace that was only used by "inferior races and social deviants."

This was not the only movement in U.S. history that sought to curb alcohol or drug use for discriminatory reasons. In 1875, for example, lawmakers in San Francisco passed a law against opium that specifically targeted smoked opium, which tended to be a Chinese custom, but left alone other forms of opium that Caucasians preferred.

ounces of pot faced a minimum of 15 years to life in prison, and a maximum of 25 to life. In 2009, New York revised its laws to remove mandatory minimum sentences. Five years later, Governor Andrew Cuomo announced plans to allow limited use of medical marijuana, giving only 20 hospitals permission to prescribe it.

Although states are slowly changing their laws, it is still a federal crime to possess and sell marijuana. Yet many people are pushing to legalize the drug across the board, especially at the federal level. In 2015 the *New York Times* shocked many when it published an editorial calling on Congress to lift the federal ban on marijuana, just as Congress reversed its decision on banning alcohol in the 1920s. "There is honest debate among scientists about the health effects of marijuana," the editorial board wrote, "but we believe that the evidence is overwhelming that addiction and dependence are relatively minor problems, especially compared with alcohol and tobacco. Moderate use of marijuana does not appear to pose a risk for otherwise healthy adults."

ARGUMENTS FOR DECRIMINALIZATION

Proponents of decriminalization cite many reasons why marijuana use should not incur legal penalties. Chief among them are the drug's medicinal qualities. As discussed in chapter one, people have used marijuana to treat a variety of maladies for thousands of years. In fact, more than 70 years ago, a person in the United States could buy more than two dozen medicines containing marijuana, many from perfectly legitimate pharmaceutical companies.

A pro-marijuana parade in Minneapolis in 2013. NORML stands for National Organization for the Reform of Marijuana Laws.

Although the Controlled Substances Act of 1970 proclaimed that marijuana had no medicinal value, the National Academy of Sciences' Institute of Medicine begged to differ. The Academy concluded in 1999 that there were "limited circumstances in which we recommend smoking marijuana for medical uses." In the minds of many doctors, marijuana is a safe, largely benign substance with many therapeutic applications. It can ease the pain and symptoms of many maladies, such as:

- controlling muscle spasms and limiting the pain caused by multiple sclerosis, which affects the brain and spinal cord
- relieving nausea from cancer chemotherapy
- relieving chronic pain
- increasing appetite and stemming weight loss
- reducing pressure within the eye caused by glaucoma, a leading cause of blindness
- preventing seizures in some patients who suffer from epilepsy

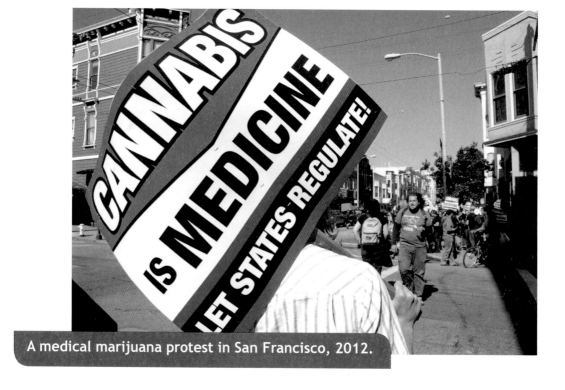

A medical marijuana protest in San Francisco, 2012.

During Operation Trident, narcotics officers from multiple agencies arrested more than 100 people and seized almost half a million marijuana plants from public lands in California.

AIDS activists were important players in the push to liberalize medical marijuana laws. The drug helped AIDS patients combat loss of appetite, nausea, headaches, and pain associated with drugs used to treat and prevent infections. These medications can cause various gastrointestinal problems and lead to the so-called AIDS wasting syndrome, which can cause a person to starve to death.

In addition to its use as a medicine, supporters of decriminalization believe the social costs of marijuana enforcement are enormous. According to the Federal Bureau of Investigation, 658,000 people were arrested for marijuana possession in 2012, compared with 256,000 arrests for cocaine, heroin, and their derivatives. Most marijuana arrests, however, disproportionally fell on the African American community. Supporters of decriminalization say blacks suffer the most because marijuana laws are inequitably enforced. Over a span of 15 years, police departments across the United States made some 10 million arrests for marijuana possession. Most of those arrests were in urban areas where African Americans tend to live.

The American Civil Liberties Union (ACLU) reported that police are 3.7 times more likely to arrest blacks for marijuana possession than whites. The ACLU said the **disparities** are "as staggering in the Midwest as in the Northeast, in large counties as in small, on city streets as on country roads. . . . They exist regardless of whether blacks make up 50% or 5% of a county's overall population."

Blacks are arrested more often than whites for marijuana-related crimes even though data suggest that young white adults (age 18 to 25) use marijuana more often than young black adults. Moreover, many of those arrested for marijuana-related crimes, whether African American or otherwise, can expect to spend a lot of time in jail if convicted.

In 1993, Jeff Mizanskey was arrested in Missouri for buying five pounds of marijuana. He was sentenced to life in prison without the opportunity of parole. "I think twenty years is more than enough," his son told a reporter in 2013. "My dad never hurt anybody. He never killed anybody. He made some mistakes, but he's paid more than enough." Mizanskey was finally released in 2015, but he is far from the only person to feel the sting of harsh pot laws. In 2010, one truck driver with a small amount of marijuana in his pocket was stopped by police in New Orleans. He was later sentenced to 13.3 years of hard labor.

Proponents of decriminalization say enforcing marijuana laws is not cost-effective. According to the ACLU, it costs local communities more than

POT AND THE UNITED NATIONS

In the fall of 2015, word leaked out that the United Nations Office on Drugs and Crime would recommend that member nations decriminalize marijuana. The agency said it was only "reviewing" the issue, although any recommendation would have no legal weight. Another UN agency, the World Health Organization, however, called for decriminalization in 2014.

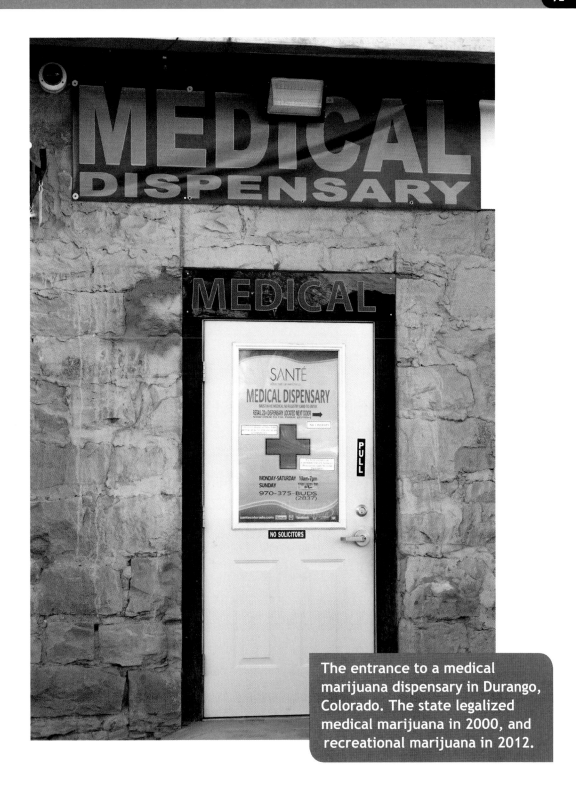

The entrance to a medical marijuana dispensary in Durango, Colorado. The state legalized medical marijuana in 2000, and recreational marijuana in 2012.

$3.6 billion a year to enforce the laws, as police, judges, prosecutors, and public defenders spend an undue amount of time and resources dealing with mostly minor possession cases. Experts say that if police are spending too much time arresting nonviolent marijuana users, they have less time to go after more dangerous and serious criminals. In the end, criminalization has not decreased the overall usage of the drug. Around 30 million Americans use marijuana every year.

ARGUMENTS FOR AND AGAINST LEGALIZATION

Decriminalization is different from legalization. Decriminalization means that while pot is still illegal, a person will not be prosecuted for possessing small amounts. Meanwhile, legalization means that it is no longer illegal to possess or use marijuana, and that its use can be fully regulated by the government.

In states or countries that have legalized marijuana, the government benefits from the sale of marijuana. Legalizing the drug gives the states the right to collect taxes and fees. In November 2015, Colorado collected $11.2 million in marijuana-related taxes and fees, up from $7.6 million a year before. In 2014 the state collected $36. 5 million. From January to November 2015, the state took in $59.7 million, well ahead of the previous year.

While supporters of legalization have waged a slow but successful campaign to liberalize or eradicate marijuana laws in many states, opponents have been equally vocal in opposition to these changes. Most of their arguments **coalesce** around the health effects of the drug. While THC has been found to have some medicinal value, recent scientific studies suggest that the dangers from marijuana outweigh its benefits. Opponents of legalization say that marijuana is addictive and that long-term use has negative consequences, especially for teenagers.

To back this claim up, opponents cite several research papers, including a 2000 study in the journal *Experimental and Clinical Psychopharmacology*. In that report, researchers concluded that marijuana was addictive. They reported that 60 percent of the people they studied had physical withdrawal symptoms after they stopped using the drug. Such symptoms are associated with addiction.

A second study undertaken by scientists at NIDA demonstrated that when researchers gave laboratory animals access to THC, the animals self-administered the cannabinoid in doses equivalent to those used by humans. Self-administering a drug is an example of drug-seeking behavior—another indication of addiction.

Although the addictive qualities of marijuana have been debated for years, opponents of legalization say cannabis use can impair a person's ability to drive, operate machinery, or study. They also say marijuana

In Roma, Texas, a border patrol agent stands by the Rio Grande River; this part of the river is often used to get drugs, especially pot, into the United States.

smoke contains the same cancer-causing chemicals as tobacco smoke. And they point out that scientists have linked marijuana with various psychiatric disorders.

Many are concerned that legalization efforts will make kids view marijuana in a more positive light. In Colorado, for example, where recreational marijuana is legal, a state survey showed that the percentage of teens who view pot as dangerous is dropping. In 2011, 58 percent of Colorado teens viewed marijuana as a risky drug. That number dropped to 54 percent in 2013. (Other studies have shown that marijuana legislation hasn't made U.S. teens more likely to use pot.)

Some people say the legalization effort is moving too fast. States might not yet have the right laws and legal guidance in place to make marijuana legal. For example, if the police pull someone over for driving under the influence of alcohol, there are clear legal limits as to when police can

The American Medical Association is against legalization, stating that marijuana is "the most common illicit drug involved in drugged driving, particularly in drivers under the age of 21."

arrest that person. No such limits exist for driving under the influence of marijuana, making it difficult for police to know when to arrest someone.

While marijuana's impact on health provides opponents of legalization ample ammunition, others fear legalization will create a new industry similar to "Big Tobacco" that will market and sell pot to children. They also fear marijuana use will increase because the drug will be easily available, just as cigarettes are. Opponents point to the Netherlands, which formally resolved to not enforce its pot laws in 1976. Within 10 years, marijuana use had grown by 300 percent due to aggressive marketing and society's shifting attitudes toward the drug.

TEXT-DEPENDENT QUESTIONS

1. How many states have liberalized their marijuana laws?
2. Name three reasons why people say marijuana should be legalized.
3. Name three reasons why people say marijuana should not be legalized.

RESEARCH PROJECT

Write an editorial either in favor of legalization or against it. Use the arguments listed in this chapter to start your research, but do some additional research to find facts to support your view.

WORDS TO UNDERSTAND

ambiguities: situations in which something can be understand in more than one way.

intervention: an action that is taken, especially to improve a particular situation such as a health problem.

paranoid: a fretful mental state in which people believe they are being plotted against by outside forces.

precedes: something that comes before something else.

psychosis: a mental disorder in which a person loses all contact with reality.

tolerance: needing more of a drug to achieve the same effect.

CHAPTER FOUR

ADDICTION AND TREATMENT

Some people love the relaxing effects of marijuana. Some claim it calms them down, while others say it makes them more creative. Others simply plop down on the couch, open a bag of snacks, and watch television. Pot makes some people less angry, while others become manic. Some suffer panic attacks, while others become **paranoid**.

But does marijuana make a user's body so dependent on the drug that a person physically can't stop using it? Is pot addictive? While some drugs, such as heroin and cocaine, offer no **ambiguities** as to whether they have addictive qualities, marijuana is much more complicated.

ADDICTION AND DEPENDENCY

Addiction is characterized by an inability to stop using a drug. The mind craves the drug's effects, and getting the drug becomes central to the addict's life. A person who is addicted to a drug will do anything to obtain

A marijuana plant being grown indoors.

it. They might lie, steal, or commit crimes. For a drug to be classified as addictive, a substantial number of users have to fail repeatedly in their attempts to stop using. Moreover, users would have to become preoccupied in obtaining the drug and use it more than they intend to.

Dependency is a hallmark sign of an addictive drug. There are two components to dependency: physical and psychological (or mental). As people become physically dependent on a drug, their bodies develop a **tolerance** to it. As the body adapts, it requires more of the drug to achieve the same effects. For example, opioids such as heroin can cause severe physical dependency. When people who are physically dependent on a drug stop using it, they will often have withdrawal symptoms. They might sweat profusely, shake, have difficulty breathing, or even hallucinate.

Mentally, a person might start to believe they need the drug to function. They will continue to use it even though it is causing problems

TEEN MARIJUANA CHECK-UP

The Teen Marijuana Check-Up program, a brief **intervention** developed by researchers at the University of Washington, is one example of *motivational enhancement therapy* at work. The idea behind the program is not to judge or wag a finger at a student who smokes pot. Counselors simply talk to the students, providing them with the myths and facts about marijuana use. The students are also educated about the various risks to their health.

The Teen Marijuana Check-Up program is offered as a free, nonjudgmental, and confidential service for teens. It is not intended to serve as a treatment program. Researchers have seen a 20 percent decrease in marijuana use among frequent marijuana users who participated in this intervention. Researchers called the findings "encouraging."

in their lives. A person who is psychologically dependent on a drug will not overcome it by willpower alone. Such a person will deny having a problem and obsess about using the drug.

SO, IS MARIJUANA ADDICTIVE?

This brings us back to the question of whether marijuana is addictive and whether it creates dependency. For years, people believed that marijuana was not addictive. In some respects, they were right, but with a qualifier—marijuana *can* be addictive, but not in the way that heroin and cocaine are addictive.

In 1994, NIDA researchers asked more than 8,000 people between the ages of 15 and 64 about their drug use. Among those who had tried marijuana at least once, about 9 percent were diagnosed as "cannabis dependent." By contrast, 15 percent of those who had tried alcohol were deemed to be dependent on it. Rates of dependence among those who experimented

Some people who use marijuana regularly report feeling irritable and uncomfortable when they try to stop.

IS SPICE ADDICTIVE?

Although research on synthetic marijuana, or spice, has been limited, a number of researchers and medical providers have viewed addictive behaviors in those who ingest spice. One case study in 2009 by German researchers described a variety of physical withdrawal symptoms among a user of spice.

According to the researchers, a 20-year-old patient smoked spice daily for eight months. Once he was admitted to the hospital, researchers said the subject began craving spice. He also began having nightmares, sweating profusely, and developing nausea. Researchers concluded that the man had "the symptoms and signs [of] dependence syndrome. . . . The physical withdrawal syndrome closely resembles that seen in cannabis dependence."

The researchers also warned about the dangers of synthetic marijuana. "The special feature of the phenomenon 'spice' is that for the first time a synthetic drug has been commercially distributed disguised as 'herbal blend.' This must be seen as a malicious deception of the consumer."

In online support groups, many spice users describe suffering from serious withdrawal symptoms such as uncontrollable vomiting and diarrhea, loss of appetite, inability to sleep, depression, psychotic episodes, and suicidal thoughts. A number of spice users claim that withdrawing from spice is as hard as, if not harder than, withdrawing from crack, heroin, and other opiates. For instance, one spice user who identified himself as "Walter" claimed, "I have done heroin, crack, and meth; nothing was harder to kick than spice."

with other drugs were higher still: 17 percent for cocaine; 23 percent for heroin, and 32 percent for nicotine, a chemical in cigarettes. Researchers concluded that yes, marijuana addiction is a reality for some. That being said, marijuana appears to be less addictive than alcohol and nicotine, both of which are legal in the United States and many other countries.

Other studies have focused specifically on high school students. Some studies have found that even though many high school students have tried marijuana, most do not develop a dependency. However, a 2002 study by the U.S. Department of Health and Human Services concluded that the *earlier* a person begins using marijuana, the *more likely* they are to become physically dependent. Rates of dependence go up to 17 percent among those who start using marijuana in their teens, and up to 25 to 50 percent among daily users. Those with a family history of substance use and mental health problems are more at risk. Moreover, many people say marijuana is more addictive today than in the past because of the rising levels of THC in cannabis.

The majority of marijuana users will not experience full-blown dependency, but most will experience withdrawal symptoms when they stop using the drug. Common withdrawal symptoms include decrease in appetite, sleeplessness, and physical discomfort. Many marijuana users report feeling irritable or moody when they stop using the drug. These symptoms are not life threatening, but they may be uncomfortable enough to make people go back to using marijuana.

A "GATEWAY DRUG?"

One of the most common concerns is that marijuana is a "gateway drug." In other words, once a person gets used to smoking pot, he or she is more likely to then try "harder" drugs such as LSD, heroin, and cocaine. Like marijuana addiction, the gateway theory needs some explaining.

Over the years, numerous studies have pointedly shown that those who use LSD, cocaine, and heroin had previously used marijuana. In 1999

Marijuana use is associated with the use of other drugs, but that does not mean that marijuana use causes other kinds of drug use.

POT, PSYCHOSIS, AND SCHIZOPHRENIA

Schizophrenia is a severe mental disorder that involves a break between a person's perception of reality and what is actually happening. Evidence suggests that teenagers who use marijuana regularly have an increased risk of developing the condition, or some other **psychosis**, later in life.

A 2011 study of nearly 2,000 teens found that those who smoked pot were twice as likely to develop a psychosis within 10 years, compared to those who did not smoke pot. Another 2011 study found that teens who use marijuana are most at risk when they have a mother, father, sister, or brother suffering from schizophrenia or some other psychotic disorder.

The relationship between pot, psychosis, and schizophrenia is complicated. It is possible that smoking pot directly increases a person's risk of psychosis and schizophrenia. Another possibility is that a person prone to psychosis and schizophrenia may be especially attracted to marijuana and its calming properties. A third explanation is that the same genes that make someone susceptible to psychosis might make that person more prone to enjoying pot.

So what are the takeaway messages? If you experiment with pot and find yourself feeling paranoid, or you have a family member with a psychotic condition, you might want to stay away from marijuana.

the Institute of Medicine reported that people who use marijuana on a daily basis "are more likely than their peers to be extensive users of other substances."

However—and this is a big "however"—just because marijuana users are more likely to use a "harder" drug later on in life, it doesn't necessarily mean that pot *caused* them to use the other drugs.

"In the sense that marijuana use typically **precedes** rather than follows initiation into the use of other illicit drugs, it is indeed a gateway drug," researchers at National Academy of Sciences said. "However, it does not appear to be a gateway drug to the extent that it is the *cause* or even that it is the most significant predictor of serious drug abuse; that is, care must be taken not to attribute cause to association."

Part of the problem, researchers said, is that much of the data that back up the "gateway theory" do not measure dependence. Instead, the data measure use, even if only once. "Thus, they show only that marijuana users are more likely to use other illicit drugs (even if only once) than are people who never use marijuana, not that they become dependent or even frequent users," the Academy researchers said.

However, some researchers believe there is a causation effect that makes marijuana a gateway drug. One statistical study by David Fergusson, a researcher at the University of Otago in Christchurch, New Zealand, suggests

According to the national survey called Monitoring the Future, in 2014 there was a decrease in the number of teens who viewed pot as dangerous, but there was no significant increase in how many had actually used it.

THE SOCIAL EFFECTS OF POT

Although the majority of users will not become dependent on marijuana, the drug can still have a negative impact on their lives. Researchers and individual narratives have shown that marijuana use can change a person's motivation levels, cause difficulty concentrating, and result in short-term memory loss. People who use marijuana can have problems at work, in school, and in personal relationships. Pot can also lead to risky behaviors, such as unprotected sex and driving while impaired.

"I hate pot," one teacher told the blog Humans of New York. "I hate it even more than hard drugs. I've taught high school for 25 years and I hate what marijuana does to my students. . . . My students become less curious when they start smoking pot. . . . People say pot makes you more creative, but from what I've seen, it narrows my students' minds until they only reference the world in relation to the drug."

that marijuana use increases the likelihood that a person will go on to use other illicit drugs. "This association was found to be particularly strong during adolescence but declined rapidly as age increased," Fergusson's study reported. However, Fergusson could not say for certain why that happens.

Other scientists have suggested that a person's social and living environment plays a role in moving from one drug to another. In their view, people who are most vulnerable to developing a substance use disorder first begin using drugs that are readily available, such as alcohol, tobacco, and marijuana. They are also more likely to interact socially with other drug users.

TREATMENT

Marijuana treatment programs have proliferated in recent years. People who seek treatment for marijuana typically continue to use it despite experiencing a variety of physical, emotional, social, and psychological consequences. Frequently, those who seek treatment are also misusing other substances, such as alcohol, prescription drugs, or cocaine.

Like those using other drugs, marijuana users have a variety of treatments available to them:

- *Cognitive-behavioral therapy* is a form of psychotherapy that teaches people how to understand and correct their behavior.
- *Contingency management* is a different approach, in which positive rewards are given for behaviors like attending sessions or maintaining sobriety.
- *Motivational enhancement therapy* is a systematic interventionist approach designed to increase people's motivation to change their behavior. In this approach, counselors and psychotherapists will not guide a patient step-by-step through recovery. Instead, users will motivate themselves by completing certain tasks.

TEXT-DEPENDENT QUESTIONS

1. What is the gateway drug theory as it applies to marijuana?
2. What are the differences between drug addiction and dependency?
3. What is motivational enhancement therapy?

RESEARCH PROJECT

Design a survey to gather information about students' opinions and attitudes about marijuana. Come up with a list of about 10 questions. Next, create a method for distributing the survey and tallying the results. Determine how many people are to be surveyed (about 20 should be appropriate). Share your findings with the class.

FURTHER READING

BOOKS AND ARTICLES

Berlatsky, Noah, ed. *Marijuana*. Opposing Viewpoints Series. Farmington Hills, MI: Greenhaven, 2012.

Goodwin, William. *Marijuana*. Drug Education Library. San Diego, CA: Lucent, 2002.

Hill, Kevin P. *Marijuana: The Unbiased Truth about the World's Most Popular Weed*. Center City, MN: Hazelden, 2015.

Jensen, Taylor S. *Understanding Drugs and Drug Addiction*. Vol. 5, *Marijuana Edition*. Lexington, KY: JK Publishing, 2012.

ONLINE

Foundation for a Drug-Free World. "The Truth about Marijuana." http://www.drugfreeworld.org/drugfacts/marijuana.html.

National Institute on Drug Abuse. "DrugFacts: Marijuana." http://www.drugabuse.gov/publications/drugfacts/marijuana.

WebMD. "How Does Marijuana Affect You?" http://www.webmd.com/mental-health/addiction/marijuana-use-and-its-effects.

EDUCATIONAL VIDEOS

Access these videos with your smartphone or use the URLs below to find them online.

"CNN Marijuana Legalization Debate," CNN. "Don Lemon of CNN hosts a passionate debate between two leading experts on marijuana legalization."
https://youtu.be/4XKhlJ6U_Rw

"Dangers of Smoking Marijuana," Teen Kids News. "Marijuana is a depressant and a White House report suggests that teens that use the drug may seriously impact their mental health in a negative way."
https://youtu.be/MY5LUcvORaM

"Debate Around Medical Marijuana." CNN. "Dr. Sanjay Gupta addresses the controversy around the use of medical marijuana." https://youtu.be/cFY6IgPgyB8

"Pot Does this to your Brain," D News (a YouTube channel about "mind-bending" facts). "Have you ever wondered what exactly marijuana does to your brain?"
https://www.youtube.com/watch?v=-hOCqQVPIzo

"Synthetic Marijuana, Real problem: Families speak out," RT America. "This video brings the real stories of three families dealing with consequences of synthetic marijuana."
https://youtu.be/qAdagCFtzXY

SERIES GLOSSARY

abstention: actively choosing to not do something.

acute: something that is intense but lasts a short time.

alienation: a sense of isolation or detachment from a larger group.

alleviate: to lessen or relieve.

binge: doing something to excess.

carcinogenic: something that causes cancer.

chronic: ongoing or recurring.

cognitive: having to do with thought.

compulsion: a desire that is very hard or even impossible to resist.

controlled substance: a drug that is regulated by the government.

coping mechanism: a behavior a person learns or develops in order to manage stress.

craving: a very strong desire for something.

decriminalized: something that is not technically legal but is no longer subject to prosecution.

depressant: a substance that slows particular bodily functions.

detoxify: to remove toxic substances (such as drugs or alcohol) from the body.

ecosystem: a community of living things interacting with their environment.

environment: one's physical, cultural, and social surroundings.

genes: units of inheritance that are passed from parent to child and contain information about specific traits and characteristics.

hallucinate: seeing things that aren't there.

hyperconscious: to be intensely aware of something.

illicit: illegal; forbidden by law or cultural custom.

inhibit: to limit or hold back.

interfamilial: between and among members of a family.

metabolize: the ability of a living organism to chemically change compounds.

neurotransmitter: a chemical substance in the brain.

paraphernalia: the equipment used for producing or ingesting drugs, such as pipes or syringes.

physiological: relating to the way an organism functions.

placebo: a medication that has no physical effect and is used to test whether new drugs actually work.

predisposition: to be more inclined or likely to do something.

prohibition: when something is forbidden by law.

recidivism: a falling back into past behaviors, especially criminal ones.

recreation: something done for fun or enjoyment.

risk factors: behaviors, traits, or influences that make a person vulnerable to something.

sobriety: the state of refraining from alcohol or drugs.

social learning: a way that people learn behaviors by watching other people.

stimulant: a class of drug that speeds up bodily functions.

stressor: any event, thought, experience, or biological or chemical function that causes a person to feel stress.

synthetic: made by people, often to replicate something that occurs in nature.

tolerance: the state of needing more of a particular substance to achieve the same effect.

traffic: to illegally transport people, drugs, or weapons to sell throughout the world.

withdrawal: the physical and psychological effects that occur when a person with a use disorder suddenly stops using substances.

INDEX

ABOUT THE AUTHOR

John Perritano is an award-winning journalist, writer, and editor from Southbury CT., who has written numerous articles and books on a variety of subjects including science, sports, history, and culture for such publishers as Mason Crest, National Geographic, Scholastic and Time/Life. His articles have appeared on Discovery.com, Popular Mechanics.com and other magazines and Web sites. He holds a Master's Degree in American History from Western Connecticut State University.

ABOUT THE ADVISOR

Sara Becker, Ph.D. is a clinical researcher and licensed clinical psychologist specializing in the treatment of adolescents with substance use disorders. She is an Assistant Professor (Research) in the Center for Alcohol and Addictions Studies at the Brown School of Public Health and the Evaluation Director of the New England Addiction Technology Transfer Center. Dr. Becker received her Ph.D. in Clinical Psychology from Duke University and completed her clinical residency at Harvard Medical School's McLean Hospital. She joined the Center for Alcohol and Addictions Studies as a postdoctoral fellow and transitioned to the faculty in 2011. Dr. Becker directs a program of research funded by the National Institute on Drug Abuse that explores novel ways to improve the treatment of adolescents with substance use disorders. She has authored over 30 peer-reviewed publications and book chapters and serves on the Editorial Board of the *Journal of Substance Abuse Treatment*.

PHOTO CREDITS